W9-DGF-656

169301

Excel Local Public Library

FEARSOME, SCARY, AND CREEPY ANIMALS

Creepy Spiders

Elaine Landau

Enslow Publishers, Inc.

40 Industrial Road   PO Box 38
Box 398   Aldershot
Berkeley Heights, NJ 07922   Hants GU12 6BP
USA   UK

http://www.enslow.com

Grand Island Public Library

Copyright © 2003 by Elaine Landau

All rights reserved.

No part of this book may be reproduced by any means
without the written permission of the publisher.

Library of Congress Cataloging-in-Publication Data

Landau, Elaine.
    Creepy spiders / Elaine Landau.
        p. cm. — (Fearsome, scary, and creepy animals)
    Summary: Introduces spiders and why they sometimes attack humans, and
tells of some real-life spider attacks.
    Includes bibliographical references (p.   ).
    ISBN 0-7660-2059-2 (hardcover : alk. paper)
    1. Spiders—Juvenile literature. 2. Poisonous spiders—Juvenile
literature. 3. Spider bites—Juvenile literature. [1. Spiders. 2.
Poisonous spiders. 3. Spider bites.] I. Title. II. Series.
QL458.4 .L34 2003
595.4'4165—dc21

                        2002006940

Printed in the United States of America

10 9 8 7 6 5 4 3 2 1

To Our Readers: We have done our best to make sure all Internet addresses in this book were active and appropriate
when we went to press. However, the author and the publisher have no control over and assume no liability for the
material available on those Internet sites or on other Web sites they may link to. Any comments or suggestions can be
sent by e-mail to comments@enslow.com or to the address on the back cover.

Illustration Credits: © 1999 Artville, LLC, pp. 30 (bottom), 31 (bottom), 33 (center); © Corel Corporation, pp.
5 (background), 16, 17, 39; Adam Hart-Davis/Science Photo Library, p. 34; David Liebman, pp. 7, 8, 9, 11, 13
(background), 22–23 (background), 24, 26–27 (background), 30 (background and inset), 31 (background), 36; Dr.
John Brackenbury/Science Photo Library, p. 14; George Andrejko/Associated Press, p. 10; Hemera Technologies,
Inc., pp. ii, iii, 5 (top), 13 (bottom), 19, 22 (bottom), 25, 26 (bottom), 37, 38; Jack Bassman, p. 23; Jamél S.
Sandidge, pp. 21, 33 (inset); John Bavaro, p. 4; Krista Widman, pp. 15, 18; Mark Clarke/Science Photo Library,
p. 12; Painet, Inc., pp. 20, 31 (inset); Pascal Goetgheluck/Science Photo Library, p. 29; PhotoDisc, pp. 4–5
(background), 6; Ruth Cotten, p. 24. Borders are from PhotoDisc.

Cover Illustration: Mark Clarke/Science Photo Library

604-J
c.2

Contents

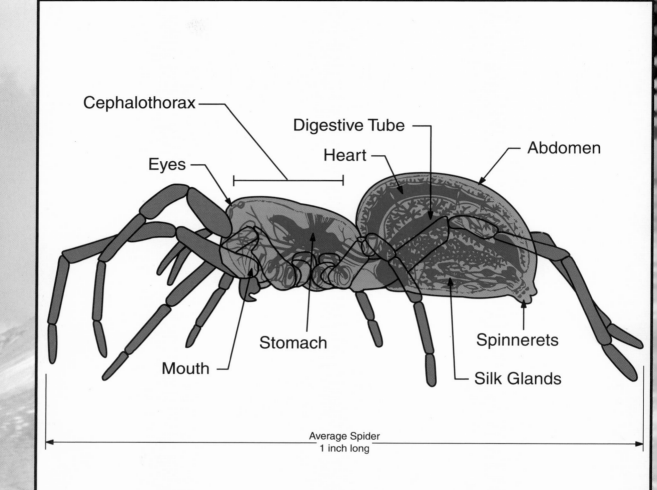

Cephalothorax

Digestive Tube

Heart

Abdomen

Eyes

Stomach

Mouth

Spinnerets

Silk Glands

Average Spider
1 inch long

Many people believe that spiders are insects, but they are not. They are small, eight-legged animals. All spiders have fangs, and most are poisonous. Very few spiders are harmful to humans, however.

1. A Scary Day

May 18, 1980 was an unforgettable day for many in Washington state. The volcano Mount St. Helens erupted. Its top was nearly blown away. There was a huge landslide. Chunks of earth came tumbling down. Forests were flattened. Lakes were filled with hot, thick volcanic ash.

Nearly sixty people died. Many more had to leave their homes. They fled to shelters. Everyone was concerned with safety.

Travelers in the area were also in trouble. They could not continue on their way. They had to stop at shelters, too. JoAnne Hahn was on the road that day. She had been in a bowling tournament, or contest, in Spokane, Washington. She was heading home to Port Orchard, Washington. But it was not safe to go on.

Driving was nearly impossible. Ash from the volcano

5

Mount St. Helens is a volcano in Washington.

was everywhere. A red haze hung in the air. Hahn later said of the eruption, "I really wasn't sure what it was. I thought it was the end of the world."

Hahn stopped at the town of Ritzville. That is about 56 miles from Spokane. She went to a shelter that was set up in an elementary school. Hahn thought that was the safe thing to do. She had no idea of what awaited her there.

By the time she arrived, JoAnne Hahn was tired. She was also covered in gray volcanic ash. She asked to take a shower. There was one at the school. But Hahn unknowingly made a terrible mistake. She happened to reach above the shower stall. She never dreamed that there was a black widow spider there—the most poisonous spider in North America. Hahn had disturbed it, and the spider bit her.

Before long, Hahn felt sick. She had trouble breathing. Her upper arm hurt badly. She was taken to the Ritzville Hospital. Two doctors and two nurses took care of her there.

Hahn thought that she might be having a heart attack. This is not uncommon. Sometimes a black widow's bite feels like a heart attack. The pain spreads up the person's arm. There is often chest pain. The victim becomes flushed and sweaty. It may be hard to breathe.

Black widow spiders do not usually attack humans, but they will when they feel threatened.

Doctors are not always sure about these bites. Some patients never see the spider. The bite wound may be tiny. Often it cannot be spotted without a magnifying glass. Different patients also react differently to the spider's poison. The amount of venom, or poison, received can make a difference. How deep the bite is matters, too.

Black widow spiders can be identified by reddish marks on their undersides.

Not all people feel like they are having a heart attack. Some have painful leg cramps or pain and stiffness in the abdomen. Their eyelids may become swollen. The soles of their feet may hurt, too. It is easy to mistake a black widow's bite for another medical problem. However, many patients claim it was the worst pain they ever felt.

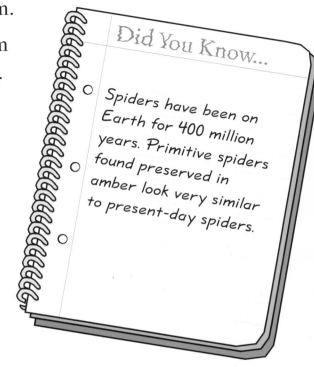

Did You Know...

Spiders have been on Earth for 400 million years. Primitive spiders found preserved in amber look very similar to present-day spiders.

The doctors at Ritzville Hospital knew that Hahn had been bitten. She was treated for the bite. The next morning, she woke up in the hospital. She already felt much better. Later, she joked about it. She said that she wanted a special T-shirt—one that said, "I survived Mount St. Helens and a black widow spider bite."

JoAnne Hahn was lucky. The black widow spider is widely feared. Its venom is fifteen times stronger than a rattlesnake's. Some people become very ill from its bite. Yet few—less than one percent of people who are bitten—die. That is because they only receive a small dose (amount) of venom.

Nevertheless, older people are more likely to have serious problems. JoAnne Hahn was a grandmother when she was bitten. Children are also at greater risk. One two-year-old boy was bitten in a garden. He had been walking barefoot there with his grandfather. Neither saw a spider. But the boy said his big toe hurt. Soon after, he

Rattlesnake venom (poison) is dangerous, but a black widow spider's poison is fifteen times stronger.

fainted. The child never came to. He was dead within the hour.

Later, his grandfather went back to the garden. He stopped where they had been. Beside a large rock was a black widow spider. It had been hidden from view. The child must have brushed against it.

People are often afraid of spiders. Some find them scary looking. They call them "creepy crawlers." Yet many spiders are helpful. They eat harmful insects, like locusts. Locusts destroy farm crops. Spiders also eat flies and mosquitoes. These insects carry disease.

Most spiders are poisonous. But they are usually not harmful to

Spiders eat locusts, which can be harmful to crops. This is a locust with a black widow spider.

humans. This is because they cannot pierce, or bite through, human skin, or because they only release a small amount of venom.

However, a few spiders can be dangerous. These spiders do not look especially frightening, but their bite should not be taken lightly. They can be scary. This is a book about some of those scary spiders. You will learn about them within these pages.

Some people are afraid of spiders. This fear is known as arachnophobia.

2. All About Spiders

Many people think that spiders are insects. This is not true. Spiders are really animals. They belong to an animal group known as arachnids. Ticks and mites are arachnids, too. Arachnids have eight legs. Insects only have six.

Most people think they know what a spider looks like. However, not all spiders look alike. Spiders may be thin, fat, or flat. Most are brown, black, or gray. But there are some very brightly colored spiders, too.

Nevertheless, there are some spider basics. Every spider's body has two sections, or parts. The front part of the spider is called the cephalothorax. This is made up of the spider's head and chest. The back of the spider

Some spiders, like this orb weaver, are colorful.

is its abdomen. A slim waist connects these two body parts.

Spiders are spineless. That does not mean they are afraid! They just do not have spines. They have no bones at all. Instead, spiders have a tough outer skin. The spider's skin protects its body. It acts as a sort of outer skeleton. Some spiders are also quite hairy.

Spiders are predators. They prey on (kill and eat) insects. Some spiders eat other small animals, too. Many spiders catch their prey in webs. They weave these webs with spider silk. This silk forms in the spider's silk glands. All spiders have three or more silk glands. They are in the spider's abdomen. Each gland gives off a different type of silk. Sometimes, the silk is quite sticky. That makes it perfect for catching and trapping bugs!

The spider uses spinnerets to spin its silk. These are sort of like spider fingers. Most spiders have six spinnerets. But some have two or four. The spinnerets are connected to the spider's abdomen.

After spinning its web, the spider waits for its prey. Some spiders wait at the center of the web. Others hide nearby. Before long, an insect will get caught in the

Spiders catch and eat insects. This black widow is eating a stink bug.

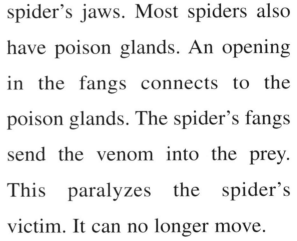

web. Some spiders do not eat their prey right away. Instead, they wrap the prey tightly in silk. This keeps it from escaping. The spider will have this meal later.

When hungry, the spider bites its prey. It uses its two sharply pointed fangs for this. These are just above the spider's jaws. Most spiders also have poison glands. An opening in the fangs connects to the poison glands. The spider's fangs send the venom into the prey. This paralyzes the spider's victim. It can no longer move.

Spiders are meat eaters, but they do not have teeth. That is because spiders do not eat solid food. They suck the body fluid out of their prey.

Spiders can also eat some of

Spiders produce silk, which they then spin into webs to trap their prey.

their prey's body tissues. They use special digestive juices for this. The spider gives off these juices when it is hungry. It sprays them on its food. The juices are very strong. They break down the prey's tissue. The tissue dissolves, or comes apart. Then, the spider sucks it up.

Spiders paralyze their prey with venom and then suck out the body fluid.

All spiders trap their prey. But they do not all use webs. There are also hunting spiders. These spiders hide and wait quietly for their prey. Then, they pounce on their victim.

Hunting spiders can see well for short distances. This is important. It helps them find and catch their prey. Most spiders have eight eyes. These are usually in two rows. Each row has four eyes. With all those eyes, you would think that spiders have great vision. But web spinners have very poor eyesight. They have to rely on their webs. Their victims have to find them!

People do not get caught in spider webs, and spiders do not hunt humans. But, at times, people are still bitten. Some spiders deliver a powerful poisonous bite. These include the black widow, the brown recluse, and the hobo spiders. Here is a closer look at each.

Black Widow

The adult black widow spider is shiny and black. Its abdomen is very round. The female has a special mark on the underside of her abdomen. It is shaped like an hourglass. The hourglass may be either red or yellow. Male black widows do not have this mark. They have light streaks on their abdomens.

Female black widow spiders have hourglass-shaped marks on their underside.

Female black widows are about 1½ inches long with their legs extended (spread open). Males are smaller than females by about half. Only the female is dangerous to humans. But these spiders would usually rather hide than bite. They only bite if they are cornered or if their webs are touched.

Brown Recluse Spider (Also Known as the Fiddleback or Violin Spider)

You can guess this spider's color from its name. Brown recluse spiders are usually brown. Some are a yellowish-tan. Others are dark brown. This spider's abdomen is often lighter than the rest of its body. The brown recluse also has a special mark on its body. The mark is shaped like a violin. That is why it is sometimes called the fiddleback or violin spider.

Brown recluse spiders vary in size. Their bodies

Brown recluse spiders are usually brownish in color.

measure from ¼ inch to ½ inch. They are bigger with their legs spread open. Some can be about the size of a dime. Others can be as big as a quarter.

In some ways, the brown recluse is like the black widow. It will bite if trapped. It will also bite if pressed against human skin.

Hobo Spider

The hobo spider is fairly large. Its body can be ¾ inch long. It is 1½ inches with its legs spread, or about as big as a silver dollar.

The hobo is brownish-gray colored. It has a V-shaped marking on its abdomen. This is called a chevron pattern. The female hobo's abdomen is larger and rounder than the male's.

Hobo spiders are also called aggressive house

spiders. Aggressive means "fierce" or "quick to attack." Sometimes, these spiders seem to run toward humans. That makes them look aggressive. But they may not be.

Hobo spiders move quite speedily. Yet they have very poor eyesight. They cannot see more than a foot or two away. So rapidly moving toward a person may not mean that the spider is bold—it just might not know where it is headed!

Hobo spiders move very quickly.

3. Really Bad Bites

Sometimes, spider bites really mean trouble. That is how it was for Ruth. She was living in Virginia when she was bitten. She was out mowing her lawn and had just cut the grass around a woodshed when it happened. She felt a pain in her right leg. At first, she did not worry. Ruth thought the mower must have hit a rock that bounced up.

But that was not so. A brown recluse spider had bitten Ruth twice. The bites were right next to each other. By that evening, her leg had begun to ache badly. Ruth found the spider's bite marks, but she did not know what they were. She thought that they were just harmless bug bites.

Soon, things worsened. Ruth described what happened this way, "Within a couple of days, the two bites became holes . . . after

22

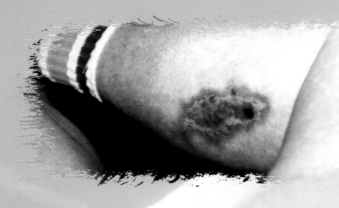

Brown recluse bites can be very dangerous, even when treated promptly. Jack Bassman (above) was bitten in 1986. Today, a large scar remains where much of his calf muscle was removed.

about a week the two holes became one big hole."

This is not unusual in a brown recluse spider bite. The spider's venom destroys human tissue. It causes the skin to rot away. Often, a blister forms at the bite site. The blister is surrounded by redness and swelling. Before long, the blister breaks open. It becomes an ulcer. An ulcer is an open, painful sore. At times, these wounds can measure ten inches in diameter. Some people also have other symptoms (signs of illness). These include fever, nausea, headaches, and body aches.

In days, the skin around the bite area darkens and then turns black as the tissue dies. In some cases, the ulcer becomes infected. This increases the amount of skin damage.

These wounds heal slowly. It may take months. Afterward, the person is left with a large scar. In many cases, surgery is needed to cut out the dead tissue.

The venom from the brown recluse spider destroys human tissue. Ruth Cotten has been suffering from this spider bite wound since 1989.

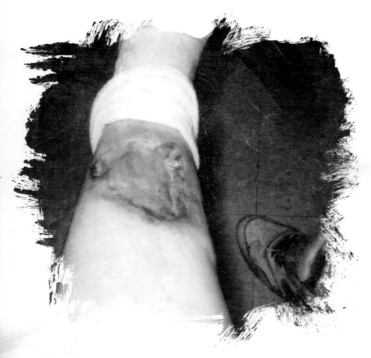

Ruth needed several surgeries. The spider's venom had badly hurt her leg. It had rotted the skin to the bone. An X-ray even showed black coloring on top of the bone. Three skin grafts were needed. In a skin graft, layers of skin are taken from another part of the body. They are transplanted, or put where there is damaged skin. It was hard for Ruth, but she made it through. Some thought she was lucky that she did not lose her leg.

The hobo spider's bite is like the brown recluse's. It also rots human tissue. Doctors often find it hard to tell the bites apart. A small number of people have died from the brown recluse's bite. Usually, these individuals did not receive medical treatment soon enough. So far, hobo spider bites have not been fatal. There have been no reported deaths.

Recently, some scientists have argued that the hobo spider's bite is not harmful to humans, after all. But this has not been proved. It is better just to keep your distance!

Did You Know...

Spiders will usually not remain in places that are constantly being cleaned. They stay in dim, cluttered areas.

4. A Special Gift

Can a harmful spider ever be helpful? The black widow once was. This spider was a sort of war hero. It happened during World War II. That was an important conflict. It lasted from 1939 to 1945. Many of the world's great powers were involved. The United States was among them.

The black widow helped the war effort. But not because of its powerful venom. It was due to its silk. Spider silk cannot be dissolved. It is the strongest natural fiber known. The black widow produces especially good silk. It is finer than a human hair, but stronger than a slim strand of steel.

The black widow's silk was used in making delicate instrument parts

Spider silk is the strongest natural fiber. It is stronger than a similarly sized strand of steel.

that were placed
in different types of
telescopes. Its silk was also
used to make some weapon parts.

Someone had to take the silk
from the spiders. That was
dangerous work, but a young
woman did it. Her name was
Armada Ruffner. Ruffner was a
civilian. She was not in the
Armed Forces. But she still
wanted to help her country.

Black widow spiders produce especially strong silk.

A spider expert worked with
Ruffner. He taught her how to
gather the silk. She would take silk from the black
widows twice a week. Every spider provided about 180
feet of silk each time.

The young woman kept her supply of black widows

in coffee cans. She fed them flies. At first, Armada Ruffner had the spiders at her home with her. But that scared her mother. So Ruffner brought them to work.

People heard about Armada Ruffner. A magazine did a story on her. She was also invited to speak on a radio show. The show was in New York City. Ruffner went there from her home in Columbus, Ohio. She

Spider silk is harvested, or collected, by spinning the silk onto a spool. The spider in this picture is a golden orb spider.

brought a jar of black widows with her.

It proved to be a scary trip, though. While in New York City, Ruffner stayed with friends. One of them made a serious mistake. Her friend took the lid off the spider jar. A black widow escaped. "There was a bit of

Did You Know...

Female black widow spiders are sometimes called "hourglass" or "shoe button" spiders because of their markings.

panic," Ruffner recalled. But things turned out all right. The spider was never found. However, no one was hurt either.

In 1945, the United States won the war. Armada Ruffner stopped working with black widows. She had done her part for America. So had the black widow spider.

5. Spiders All Around

Different types of spiders live around the world. However, the black widow, brown recluse, and hobo spiders can be found in North America. They are often spotted in the following areas:

Habitats (Where Spiders Live)

Black Widow Spiders

Black widow spiders usually live in warm regions. They are common in the desert regions of the southwestern United States. But these spiders have also been found in most states.

Black widow webs tend to lack shape or form. The spiders usually weave them near the ground. Black widows like dry, poorly lit

spots. They are often seen near woodpiles or in hollow logs. Most often, black widow spiders live outdoors. Cold weather can drive them inside, though.

Brown Recluse Spiders

Brown recluse spiders are found throughout much of south-central United States. That includes Louisiana, Mississippi, Alabama, Tennessee, and Missouri. The largest population of brown recluse spiders is found in Texas, Oklahoma, Arkansas, and Kansas. These spiders weave their webs in dark, shady places. They are common near woodpiles and sheds.

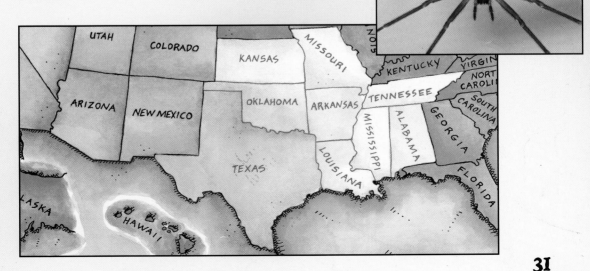

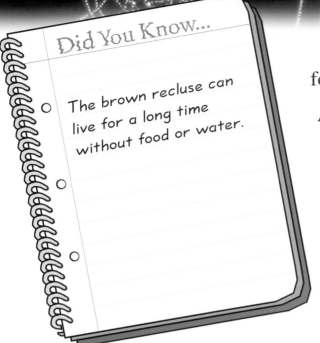

Did You Know...

The brown recluse can live for a long time without food or water.

The brown recluse is also found inside people's homes. At times, people are bitten while they sleep. The brown recluse spider climbs up to their beds on blankets that reach the floor. The brown recluse is active at night, when it hunts for prey.

Of course, the people sleeping do not know this. They often roll over onto these spiders. That is when they are bitten.

The brown recluse spider hides during the day. It seeks out dark, shadowy places. Sometimes, these spiders stay in piles of clothes. People have been bitten putting on a shirt or pants. Brown recluse spiders have even stayed in people's shoes. They bite people as they put their shoes on.

Hobo Spiders

Hobo spiders are found in the Pacific Northwest. These states include Washington, Idaho, and Oregon. They have also been found in western Montana, Nevada, northern Utah, and central and southwestern Wyoming.

Hobo spiders are not good climbers. They are usually found on the ground or in basements. Outdoors, they may be seen near the foundation (bottom) of homes, as well as near garden planters.

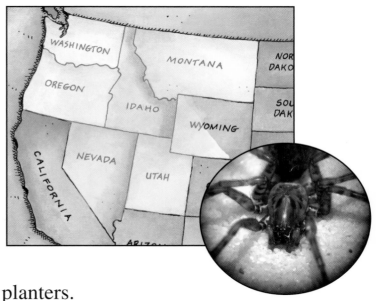

Hobo spiders build a funnel-shaped web. It looks like an open cone that narrows to a tube. The hobo spider stays at the rear of the web. This web is not sticky; the insect does not get stuck in it. Instead, the hobo spider waits for its prey to trip on the web. Then, it quickly attacks. The prey does not have a chance to get away.

Reproduction (Making More Spiders)

Male and female spiders mate to reproduce. Weeks or even months after mating, the female lays eggs. These will develop into spider young. Newborn spiders are called spiderlings.

Most female spiders keep their eggs in a small silk sac. The spider

Many poisonous animals are brightly colored as a warning to predators. When spiderlings hatch, they may be brightly colored so predators think they are poisonous and stay away.

weaves the sac herself, and the spiderlings hatch inside the sac. But they do not leave right away. First, they must molt to get bigger. When molting, a spider sheds (loses) its outer skin. A new outer skin beneath the old one replaces it. Spiderlings leave the sac one at a time. They exit through a tiny hole they tear in the sac.

There are some differences in how spiders reproduce. A few of these are described below

The egg sac of a black widow can contain up to 900 spiderlings.

Black Widow Spider

The black widows' egg sacs are about ½ inch long. These are tan colored. They feel like paper. The sacs hold from 25 to 900 eggs. These female

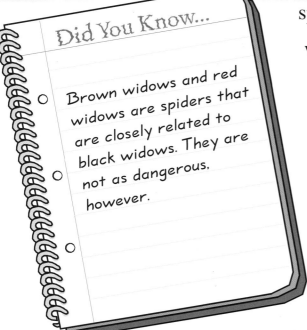

Did You Know...

Brown widows and red widows are spiders that are closely related to black widows. They are not as dangerous, however.

spiders hang the sacs in their web. The young black widows are orange and white.

The female black widow sometimes kills the male after mating. That is why it is called a "widow" spider. A widow is a woman whose husband has died.

Brown Recluse Spider

Brown recluse females keep their eggs in off-white silk sacs. The sacs are ½ inch long.

Hobo Spiders

Hobo spiders mate in late summer or early fall. Males search for females. During that time, they are seen more often. Hobo female spiders put their eggs in one to four sacs. They often attach their egg sacs to the undersides of rocks or logs.

Keep Your Distance!

The black widow, brown recluse, and hobo spiders can hurt you. So it is best to steer clear of them. These tips can help you do that.

- ❖ Do not leave the door open—not even for a minute. Spiders can come through the door before you realize that they are there.

- ❖ Any cracks or holes in walls should be filled in. Spiders can get inside a house that way.

- ❖ Do not let piles of clutter build up. This is especially important in attics, basements, and dark closets. Spiders can hide in heaps of toys and stuffed animals.

- ❖ Dust and vacuum well. Pay special attention to areas around windows or corners. Spiders can also lurk (hide) beneath furniture.

- ❖ Shake out clothing before dressing. Do the same with shoes.

Spiders can hide in piles of wood.

❖ Wear gloves when working with firewood.

Hopefully, you will never be bitten by one of these spiders. But if that ever happens, do the following:

❖ Wash the bite area with soap and water.

❖ Apply a cold compress to the area (a washcloth dipped in cold water will do). Wring it out before putting it on the bite.

❖ Keep the limb (arm or leg) that was bitten raised to prevent swelling.

❖ Seek medical help right away.

❖ Dangerous spiders are not monsters. Usually, they bite only to defend themselves. We must respect their place in nature—and it is best to respect them from a distance!

Tarantulas

Tarantulas are spiders. But they do not look like most spiders. These arachnids are large, hairy, and a bit scary-looking. Some tarantulas are among the largest spiders known. These measure between 7 and 10 inches.

There are many stories about tarantulas. People once thought a tarantula's bite caused a strange disease. Supposedly, the victim would jump over furniture. The person might also yell and run about. Of course, this was never true.

There are about 800 types of tarantulas, but the tarantulas usually found in the United States are not very dangerous. Their bite is no worse than a bee sting. Some people even keep them as pets. Yet many people would prefer not to look at them. How about you?

Fast Facts About SPIDERS

❖ Many spiders are so small that their colors and patterns can only be seen under a microscope.

❖ Some species of spiders that live in dark places have no eyes at all.

❖ Spiders have no muscles with which to extend their legs. Instead, the blood pressure in their bodies allows them to spread their legs.

❖ Some spiders can go for over a year without eating.

❖ Spider silk cannot be dissolved in water.

❖ Female tarantulas have lived for up to 20 years in captivity.

❖ Some spiderlings can travel great distances by "ballooning." They climb to the top of a tall object and let the wind pull silk threads out of their spinnerets. The spiderlings are then pulled into the air by the silk threads.

Glossary

abdomen	The lower section of a spider's body.
aggressive	Fierce or quick to attack.
arachnids	The animal group to which spiders belong.
arachnophobia	The fear of spiders.
cephalothorax	A spider's head and chest.
chevron pattern	A V-shaped design.
dose	Amount.
fangs	Long, sharp, pointed teeth.
funnel-shaped	Shaped like an open cone that narrows to form a tube.
gland	An organ in the body that produces a substance.

habitat	The place where an animal lives.
limb	A body part used to move or grasp. Arms and legs are limbs.
lurk	To stay hidden or move in a sneaky way.
mate	To come together to reproduce.
molt	The loss of an outer covering of skin.
paralyze	To cause to be unable to move.
predator	An animal that hunts other animals for food.
prey	An animal hunted and eaten by another animal.
shed	To lose or cast off.
spiderlings	Spider young.
spinnerets	The finger-like parts of a spider's body used to spin silk.
symptom	A change in the body that shows you are ill.

tournament	A contest.
transplant	To move something from one place to another.
venom	Poison.
vision	Eyesight.

Further Reading

Berger, Melvin and Berger, Gilda. *Do All Spiders Spin Webs? Questions and Answers About Spiders*. New York: Scholastic, 2000.

Berman, Ruth. *Spinning Spiders*. Minneapolis, Minn.: Lerner Publications, 1998.

Facklam, Margery. *Spiders and Their Web Sites*. Boston, Mass.: Little Brown and Company, 2001.

Fowler, Allan. *Spiders Are Not Insects*. Danbury, Conn.: Children's Press, 1996.

George, Jean Craighead. *The Tarantula In My Purse and 172 Other Wild Pets*. New York: Harper Trophy, 1997.

Gibbons, Gail. *Spiders*. New York: Holiday House, 1993.

Glaser, Linda. *Spectacular Spiders*. Brookfield, Conn:
Millbrook Press, 1998.

Llewellyn, Claire. *Spiders Have Fangs*. Brookfield,
Conn: Copper Beach Books, 1997.

Markle, Sandra. *Outside and Inside Spiders*. New York:
Bradbury Press, 1994.

Internet Addresses

Explorit Science Center: Spider Facts

This interesting Web site offers in-depth information on spiders.

<http://www.explorit.org/science/spider.html.html>

Kids Health: Hey! A Brown Recluse Spider Bit Me!

Information on the brown recluse spider, how to avoid being bitten, and what to do in the event of a spider bite.

<http://kidshealth.org/kid/ill_injure/aches/
brown_recluse.html>

Index